# Beside Still Waters

*A Journey to the heart of God*

# Beside Still Waters

*A Journey to the Heart of God*

***Celebrating the Beauty of God's Creation***

*Written and Edited by Frederick Julian Richardson*

BRENTWOOD BOOKS

Brentwood, Tennessee

Published MCMXCIII in Brentwood, Tennessee, by Brentwood Books


ISBN 1-55897-568-3


Written and edited by Frederick Julian Richardson

Design by Tal Howell Design

Project Coordinator, Jackie L. Hall

Photo credits: pp. 6-13 and 18-27 ©Paul Boothe; pp. 16-17 ©Jeff Phillips

*Scripture taken from the HOLY BIBLE, NEW INTERNATIONAL VERSION,
courtesy of the International Bible Society.*

Printed in Mexico

# *Foreword*

How thrilling and yet completely calming to think that the Creator of the universe chooses to spend intimate time conversing with us his creatures.  He calls us to himself with a still small voice and with a great magnificent landscape, with a brilliant rainbow across the sky and with a tiny leaf fluttering in the wind.

With this book you're invited to pause from the rush of our busy world, and listen for the voice of the Almighty.  In these pages you will find words from great hymns of our faith which have ministered God's grace to countless thousands through the years.  The thoughts and the pictures which accompany these words are meant to inspire you and to remind you that your heavenly Father is always willing, always waiting, always wanting to meet with you, to walk with you, to talk with you *Beside Still Waters*.

What a wonderful gift of beauty God gives us in the changing seasons. The splendor of colors in the fall leaves, the brilliant white of winter's snows, the great variety of spring's blossoms and the rich green of summer's lawns all speak to us of his love and his desire to give his children pleasure.

As we watch the seasons change he speaks to us of hope, of renewal, of old things passing away so that all may become new. May we lift to him our hymn of praise for his creative beauty around us; may we embrace the changing seasons within us.

*Thank you, Lord, for the beauty of the earth. Thank you, Lord, for my rebirth.*

# FOR THE BEAUTY
## OF THE EARTH

*For the beauty of the earth,*

*For the glory of the skies,*

*For the love which from our birth*

*Over and around us lies:*

*Lord of all, to Thee we raise*

*This our hymn of grateful praise.*

**"Then God saw everything He had made,**
**and indeed it was very good."**

*Genesis 1:31*

# HO, EVERYONE THAT IS THIRSTY

*Ho, everyone that is thirsty in spirit!*

*Ho, everyone that is weary and sad!*

*Come to the fountain; There's fullness in Jesus.*

*All that you're longing for, Come and be glad.*

**"He split the rocks in the desert and gave them water as abundant as the seas; he brought streams out of a rocky crag and made water flow down like rivers." (Ps. 78:14, 15)**

**"Jesus answered, 'Everyone who drinks this water will be thirsty again, but whoever drinks the water I give him will never thirst. Indeed, the water I give him will become in him a spring of water welling up to eternal life.'" (Jn. 4:13, 14)**

In all of our lives there are desert dry times; times in which our spirits are parched and crackled, longing for the refreshment of the water from God's river of life. What a promise we have from Jesus himself that he will quench that thirst! Not only will he quench the thirst, but he promises us that once we dip into his well he will cause the waters of eternal life to start to flow out of us. We have his assurance that we can and will be eternally refreshed; we have his blessing to become a fountain of eternal refreshment to those around us.

*Dear Lord, I come to your fountain. Please refresh my thirst; please make me a vessel through whom you can pour out your gladness.*

*I*t begins as a trickle from heaven. Slowly but surely turning away the turmoil, washing away the worry, God's perfect peace begins its flow into our lives until it lifts us up above the commonplace, out of the everyday and places us high above into the sublime.

The more we allow his peace its presence in our lives, the greater it becomes. It is a peace which has the power of a waterfall, which no obstacle can turn aside; yet with all its power, it will only wash over us with the supreme gentleness of a quiet pool.

*Almighty God, fuller every day,*

*deeper all the way —*

*may I so know your peace.*

## LIKE A RIVER GLORIOUS

*Like a river glorious, Is God's perfect peace*

*Over all victorious In its bright increase;*

*Perfect, yet it floweth Fuller ev'ry day,*

*Perfect, yet it groweth Deeper all the way.*

# WHEN MORNING GILDS THE SKIES

*When morning gilds the skies*

*My heart, awaking, cries,*

*May Jesus Christ be praised!*

*Alike at work and prayer,*

*To Jesus, I repair;*

*May Jesus Christ be praised!*

Each morning we wake up to another day. Our eyes open; we stretch our muscles to get them moving and ready for the day's work and play. We break our fast with a morning meal to give nourishment to our bodies. We chart that day's itinerary. But how do we wake up our hearts? How do we nourish our souls? How do we stretch our spiritual muscles and prepare them for their day's work? As we begin each new day, how can we get ready to navigate through the hills and valleys, the rocks and trees which could snag us and get us off of God's course for us?

"To Jesus, I repair. . ." There lies the answer. Return to Jesus. If we are broken in spirit, then he will repair us.

Jesus, the word of God, is our only source for renewed spiritual strength. As we read God's word, as we spend time with the Father in prayer, Jesus, through the Holy Spirit, promises to awaken our hearts, to give nourishment to our souls, to prepare us for anything we may need to face the day.

*Dear Lord, awaken my heart each morning, each moment of each day,*

*so that I may joyfully say "May Jesus Christ be praised!"*

## MY FAITH HAS FOUND A RESTING PLACE

*My faith has found a resting place*
*Not in device or creed;*
*I trust the Everliving One,*
*His wounds for me shall plead.*

*Home.* In meaning it is a word which is not so different from *house* or *residence, dwelling* or *abode.* A rather ordinary four-letter word. And yet what this word does in our hearts, in our memories, in our longings is so very very different from those other words with similar meanings. Home is not just a roof over our heads, not just four walls to protect us from the elements. No, home is where our emotions live, where we laugh and love, comfort and cry.

Just as each human being has an emotional longing for a place called home, so does each one of us have a spiritual longing. God has placed within us a knowledge of things eternal, a desire to seek his face. Whether we choose to fulfill the desire is up to us. And there is only one way to do that.

**"My faith has found a resting place. . ."**
And that is in Jesus Christ. Resting in Jesus. He is the fulfillment of our spiritual longing for home.

*Dear Lord, thank you for placing in me*
*the desire to be at home with you.*

# HAVEN OF REST

*I've anchored my soul*
*In the "Haven of Rest,"*
*I'll sail the wide seas no more;*
*The tempest may sweep o'er the wild, stormy deep,*
*In Jesus I'm safe evermore.*

Where are you in your life's journey?  Are you just setting out, just embarking on a new career, in a new marriage, sailing off to a new city or town?  On any new venture there are doubts and fears, but Jesus is a Haven of Rest.

Are you in the middle of life?  Are you out at sea, a warship in the midst of the battle, wondering if it is time to man the lifeboats?  In any battle it is hard to see through the fire and the smoke, but Jesus is a Haven of Rest.

Or, are you nearing the end of your journey?  Have you retired from the battle, have you finished the course, have you lost your mate?  Wherever you are sailing today, Jesus is a Haven of Rest.

*Lord, the waves are high today.  Thank you for being my haven.*

# NEAR TO THE HEART OF GOD

*There is a place of quiet rest,*

*Near to the heart of God …*

*A place where all is joy and peace,*

*Near to the heart of God.*

How often we hold God at arm's length, unwilling to allow him to lift us up onto his lap and cuddle away our concerns. Like tempestuous two-year-olds we struggle against his caring embrace, only yielding when our fear of circumstances chases us into those waiting, open arms.

Well, no matter how far away we may try to stray, he is always waiting there, always more than willing to meet us at that place, to draw us to his heart and say, *"Come to me, all you who are weary and burdened, and I will give you rest."* (Mt. 11:28)

*Dear Lord, show me that place of quiet rest;*
*draw me to your heart today.*

# THIS IS MY FATHER'S WORLD

*This is my Father's world,*
*And to my list'ning ears*
*All nature sings, and round me rings*
*The music of the spheres.*

*"Since the creation of the world God's invisible qualities —*
*his eternal power and divine nature — have been clearly seen,*
*being understood from what has been made." (Rom. 1:20)*

The wind blows through fall trees causing flaming leaves to rustle their way to the ground. What do you hear? Is it the dread call to take the rakes out of the garage and get busy with hand-blistering work? Or can you hear God calling you to take just a moment, make yourself a pillow from the tree-down, have a seat and spend some time with him?

"List'ning ears." That is the only equipment we need to receive the voice of God, the voice which speaks to us not only in a Sunday sermon, not only in our favorite Bible verse, but also in a summer midnight sky, in the delicate petals of a dusty rose, in the galloping hooves of a wild stallion. This is our Father's world, and he will use it to speak to us. With all of his creation he says, "for him who has ears to hear, let him hear." Let us all pray for listening ears.

*"God writes the gospel not in the Bible alone,*
*but on trees, and flowers, and stars." (Martin Luther)*

# IT IS WELL WITH MY SOUL

*When peace, like a river,*
*Attendeth my way,*
*When sorrows like sea*
*billows roll;*
*Whatever my lot,*
*Thou hast taught me to say,*
*It is well, it is well with my soul.*

In the cold, icy December waters of the North Atlantic in 1873, Horatio G. Spafford, a prominent Chicago lawyer, sailed on a sad mission to meet his wife in Great Britain. His family had scheduled a trip to Europe for Mrs. Spafford's health at the recommendation of their family doctor. When an unforeseen business concern forced Mr. Spafford to stay in Chicago, they decided that his wife and four daughters should leave as planned. On November 22 an English vessel collided with the ship on which the Spaffords travelled. Mrs. Spafford was quickly rescued, but all four girls were tragically lost.

As his ship neared the spot where the accident took place and Mr. Spafford looked out over the waters, he didn't ask why. He didn't shake his fist, or curse, or deny the existence of the God he had come to trust.

No, Horatio G. Spafford, the prominent Chicago lawyer, the mourning father of four precious daughters, looked out over the cold, icy December waters and wrote a hymn of faith, a hymn of hope, a hymn of affirmation of God's mighty love and compassion which has ministered to countless thousands for over one hundred years. With trust in his God he wrote *"Whatever my lot, Thou hast taught me to say, It is well, it is well, with my soul."*

**Lord, please give me the faith of Horatio Spafford. Whatever my circumstances, may I always say, "it is well, it is well with my soul."**

# WONDERFUL PEACE

*Peace!  Peace!  Wonderful peace,*

*Coming down from the Father above!*

*Sweep over my spirit forever, I pray,*

*In fathomless billows of love.*

*"And the peace of God, which transcends all understanding,*

*will guard your hearts and your minds in Christ Jesus." (Ph. 4:7)*

God's wonderful peace is always ours.  It is ours when we are in a place of tranquility, in a place of beauty and rest and comfort.

What makes it truly wonderful, however, is that it is ours when we are not in that place.  Even when it seems as though we should not have it, when it "transcends all understanding," God will give us his peace.  No matter what our minds may try and tell us, God proclaims for us peace through Jesus Christ.  The situation we are in may try and take us away from that place, and yet God sends his peace to sweep over us with his "fathomless billows of love."

That is a peace which is truly wonderful.

*Overwhelm me, Lord, with your wonderful peace.*

# GOD LEADS US ALONG

*In shady green pastures so rich and so sweet,*
*God leads His dear children along.*

**"The Lord is my shepherd, I shall not want.  He makes me lie down in**
**green pastures, he leads me beside quiet waters, he restores my soul."**
*(Ps. 23:1-3a)*

**"My sheep listen to my voice; I know them, and they follow me."**
*(Jn. 10:27)*

$\mathcal{L}$isten. Do you hear the voice of Jesus? What is he saying to you today? Perhaps he is saying, *"Be still and know that I am God;"* perhaps *"Come to me and I will give you rest;"* or maybe for you today he says *"Your eye has not seen, nor your ear heard, what I have planned for you who love me, who are called according to my purpose."*

What has he planned for those of us who love him? He leads us into green pastures where we can graze and grow strong on the nourishment of his word; he leads us beside still waters where he can restore our souls. And then, even if we go through the valley of the shadow of death, we will fear no evil. Why? Because we hear his voice.

*Lord, where you lead, I will follow.*

# ROCK OF AGES/HE HIDETH MY SOUL

*Rock of Ages, cleft for me,*

*Let me hide myself in Thee. . .*

*A wonderful Saviour is Jesus, my Lord,*

*A wonderful Saviour to me.*

*He hideth my soul in the cleft of the rock,*

*Where rivers of pleasure I see.*

Hidden in Jesus; that is our goal: To put ourselves so far into him that our self is no longer visible, no longer distinguishable from him. The nails of the cross chiselled holes into that Rock big enough for all of us, big enough for all of humanity to climb into and so hide ourselves within. "Cleft for me" the great hymn says. Yes, cleft for me and for you, for every generation before us and every generation to come.

And once we climb inside he fulfills his every promise by offering so many rivers of pleasure to see. There is the river of life in his salvation; the refreshing river of his peace; the rushing river of his joy; the quiet river of his love.

Hear him as he calls out to you today:

*Climb into the Rock and hide yourself in me.*

# IN THE GARDEN

*I come to the garden alone . . .*

*And He walks with me,*

*And He talks with me,*

*And He tells me I am His own.*

We must all walk out of our own private darkness and enter the light of his garden alone.  Though our mothers and fathers show us the way, we must go into the garden alone.  Though great men and women of God teach us the way, we must go into the garden alone.  Though we join strong, vibrant churches where people know God and desire to make him known to others, we as individuals must enter the garden alone.

But we are never left alone.  Jesus Christ awaits us there.  And once we enter his garden, then he will walk with us, no matter where we walk, and talk with us, no matter what we need to discuss, and he will assure us that we are his own forever and ever and ever.

Amen.